Sipping Tea & Bull Frog Songs

... and other sightings of the Wind Rose

A Prose & Poetry Collection

Book One: The Wandering Wonderer Series

Baidha Dominique Fercoq

ISBN: 978-81-8253-722-4
Cyberwit.net
HIG 45 Kaushambi Kunj, Kalindipuram
Allahabad – 211011 (U.P.) India
info@cyberwit.net

Author may be contacted at BaidhaFercoq@gmail.com

Dedication

To the child within, whose innocence keeps our footsteps light; may the Wind Rose fragrance be your guiding call. For you who struggle to keep that voice alive, this poetry book is for you.

To my Wind Rose, my friend, my Mother, Claudine Fercoq.

The rain cleansed the air
The cardinals are singing
A dog is barking
Nature is just waking.

The wind is tussling my hair
I am free.

Poem by Claudine

Preface

A forgotten term, the Wind Rose is an Old World map reference to cardinal points meant to guide travelers and keep them true in their journey. This rose kept unsuspecting sailors of yore from perilously falling off the edge of the world during their explorations. We might not refer to cardinal points in the same way today, but we can't dispute its orientation reliability. While modern technology minimizes the chance of turning down the wrong road, it is not very helpful in keeping us from getting lost 'figuratively' within our life. One wrong choice and our lives can be upended, causing us to spend decades undoing a momentary lapse in judgment.

It took years of wrong turns and endless spats of self-talk to realize I knew where I needed to go all along. The secret I needed to discover was allowing my mind and incessant chatter to quiet themselves enough so I could 'hear' my intuitive voice. Turns out, the best place I could minimize all that conflicting internal dialogue was within Nature – pure and simple.

In my book, I am going to propose Nature is the figurative Wind Rose we need to navigate through our life, and if allowed, she will lead us steady and true.

Book One of the Wandering Wonderer series will take the reader through all realms of nature and pose reflective questions meant to awaken dulled perceptions. This dullness is an inevitable consequence of today's modern manic drive towards consumptive distraction. Perhaps my words – like breadcrumbs – will help you in your quest to find your own True North. Let's be clear, there is no universal path for everyone's life. But perhaps these quiet, nature contemplations will help you discover the signs that will bring you closer to who and where you are meant to be.

Prose vignettes and reflective conversations surrounding nature and its creatures frame each poem within the lens of daily human experiences and struggles. Chapters focus upon specific sources of inspiration and encourage the reader to open his/her perception's aperture. I close this book with insights that surprised and inspired me during my own meandering walk through life.

May the Wind Rose return you to Nature's peace.

Table of Contents

I: Forests, Trees and Leaves

And who that approaches a forest and its living trees does not depart its presence but as a changed being? Every breath that is inhaled whirls ancient seeds of knowing; the knowing of stillness and calmness which only forests can bestow.

Each foray into the forest thicket brings new thoughts and we amaze ourselves how quickly their truths are forgotten, mindful only of the deep appreciation that comes from remembrance ... and our longing to keep such understandings within our grasp.

Walk with me through shadowed forests, thick with verdant sentries whose outstretched limbs greet us at its plush moss carpet door.

Time is a salve that offers healing, though slow in its process. We invariably struggle with traumas, physical or otherwise. During these struggles, there are things that will be lost - but there are also things that will be gained.

A Tree's Sadness

Sadness has a quality unto itself
where the bark from a tree has been torn
in a violent fashion.

The marrow of the tree's trunk
now exposed and vulnerable to insects
that harpoon their teeth
and suck life juices that sustain its growth.

The leaves droop and branches decay
while defenses mount - sacrifices must be made
to conserve life's cherished breath.

Slowly, our tree finds its strength
to stretch its leaves upward
and greet the sun.

The scar does remain, unsightly from its initial assault
but time will soften its jagged ridges
and smooth rolls will slowly find their way onto the surface.

There will come a day
when a passerby will note, almost as a second thought
"My, I wonder what did happen here."

Yet, the tree tells no story aloud
the wind blows its softened breeze
and the birds offer polite song
as our tree grows taller again
its struggle has been overcome.

How easy our minds can forget, as our thoughts become embroiled in trivial matters of every day. And these matters take on a significance that can overrule our sense of peace and connection with those around us, and with nature itself. In today's world, we often lose ourselves to such distractions over which we have no control ... and personal happiness slowly drains from us ... leaving us confounded in our discontent. It can be said Nature offers more than visual beauty when we walk within its blowing breeze, if we can only, but for a moment, be still

.

Along The Forest Path

Like a scarf unfurled
and thrown into the wind
I surrendered pieces
and then my whole.

Taking a promenade
amongst rooted cedar groves
whose bows ebbed and danced
like ocean waves in fluid flow
Ii too, cast adrift my dubious hold.

I talked of great matters
with a council of boisterous bull frogs
who convincingly expounded
of lively waters in this winter's forecast.

And the birds
what did they say?
I couldn't rightly disclose
I was lost in their melodic sail of tunes
that hijacked my thoughts
and lifted me into the breeze.

All the while
the sun painted its warming strokes upon my face
assuring me the clouds too,
would bring needed things our way.

But then again, I was distracted
while the morning dew was busy
bathing the grassy fields in pearly drops.

Nature silently travels the road of time. Often with no witness to share its unfolding, the cycle of life continues its march in solitude – leaving behind only minute evidence of yesterday's presence. There is a silent story for most of life, even a tree's life within an orchard.

An Orchard's Serenade

In a large orchard
with many rows, neatly lined
stood a tree of gnarly growth
for many generations it shared its fruit.

It wasn't pretty, it wasn't tall
but its branches stretched wide
and its leaves spread, to catch the sun
its bows would gently rock, in autumn's breeze.

Every spring, the bees would come
they would gather their gold
and spread their pollen
amongst every tree in the orchard's grounds.

This magnificent tree
with roots so deep
did bear fruit of sweetest tastes
farmers came far, to gather its fruit.

But there came a year
when the tree, did bud no more
while the bees continued their daily duty
some would rest, upon its barren branches.

And the summer, slowly crept along
while fruit fell from all the trees
our grand tree sat in silence
as the last of life, slowly decayed.

In the winter's slumber
a barren silhouette stands ... vestiges of yesterdays.

An interesting metamorphosis begins as one slowly enters a forest. We leave behind things and thoughts considered important in our lives. And as we venture deeper, we seem to find other things that surpass such notions ... and reveal to us a value of greater importance.

Ancient Bows

An overheard secret courted my ear
heralding from days bygone
old & forgotten
forest royalty of ancient growth.

When a distant unrecorded breeze
began to creak their mighty bows
causing stands unable to resist its sway
to discourse in crystal currents.

Like secret conversations
we once freely did partake
again
I am unlashed and released
causing a symphonic jubilation
to couple with my soul.

And I
all too happy to resume
this once
distant dance.

Watching the leaves during autumn and fall naturally brings forth mixed feelings. Life is filled with many paradoxes and autumn colorfully presents contrasting reflections.

Autumn's Last Dance

As the last bit of autumn's rays
kissed itself upon the leaf
the leaf falls in silent surrender.

Riding a chariot of swaying breeze
in effortless glide with softest of grace
to find its place, in a river's refuge.

The crystal waters embrace the leaf
with deliberate swiftness, the currents race.

Bit by bit, it relinquishes its grip
the leave, no more, remains afloat
graciously greeted and put to rest
amongst polished rocks on river's bed.

The only sounds remain to hear
belong to gentle breeze and babbling brook.

Another season begins to end.

The forgotten leaf will sway no more
no more casting shadows from its silhouette
to land upon the forest floor.

Consigned to lay on river's bottom
its body bows and begin to disintegrate
remains are left to nourish the earth
for another tree to spring forth again.

And on its branches, will be clothed
abundant buds will spring as leaves.

The leaf has left, and in its stead
will another cycle
spring to grow to fall and fade.

There is a melancholy that clings upon the morning's dew when autumn leaves begin their fall. Reluctance grips us in silent corners of our thoughts and yet, we are ready to embrace nature's hiatus.

Autumn's Leaf

Before I knew
autumn's leaves had fled
seeking refuge as camouflage
on earth's tired floor.

Every step I took
brought memory's conversation closer
rekindled by time's secret charm.

As the crisp breeze waltzed upon my skin
and the softened sun set its twilight
treasured rays like ribbons floating through the sky

... where is it season's time finds its nest?

Surely, life's lament
lies not in autumn's fallen leaves
for lessons past
enrich the soil.

Watching Fall approach with the sun's changing hues and its slanting rays, we reflect on the year's story. It's when the leaves begin to dot the ground below that our thoughts reflect on the temporary state of life; in flux, always changing, and never remaining static for too long.

Circles and Cycles

Leaflets, memories and leaves
they fall mostly unadorned
hostage to the breeze
their destiny unknown.

Weathered
they decompose.

Witnesses
like rings within a tree
speaking of a past now done
good years, bad years
too wet, too dry.

Indifferent to time
simply passing along.

The wonderful place of yesterday is often muted from past pain and embellished with the sun's gentle warmth. We do, as adults, so fondly reminisce and pine for playgrounds and forest fields. But in our looking back, we may also unknowingly fail to see the joy in our adult lives.

Fields of Yesterday

In the fields of yesterday
with its lingering scent
of fresh-cut grass,

where innocence's laugh
can still be heard,

where hearts ~ still open
share dreams and smiles,

that is where ~ our child remains
... in the fields of yesterday,

this story told, is not done yet
for time is neigh ~ to seek your child
bring dreams of yore, into light of day
so yet again ~ your heart may play.

I was walking in the forest this morning, stopping along the way to taste the last of blackberries ...the sunlight was sparkling just right as it bathed the trees. It was one twinkle so bright in the crisp morning air that awakened something within. I couldn't fathom humanity existing without nature; but yet, man in his activities rushes to consume all ~ leaving such vast areas of desiccated land, spewing filth into our air, draining water sources, and dismantling mountains stone by stone. My soul cried.

How Can We Ask for Pardon?

Pardon the wind
should he blow so hard
he doesn't mean to brush upon your face
in a manner as to disturb.

Pardon the rain
should she obscure your view
and cause you soggy socks
she means but to nourish the soil
and replenish streams and puddles
for nature's creatures, big or small.

Pardon the trees
should they shed upon your lawns
their sinewy spent leaves made breathable air
don't rake and cart away tomorrow's soil
thinking your lawns should be tidy and kept.

...

Pardon the man
that walks with asserted conceit
forgetting the balance
he has failed to keep.

How fragile are the things most precious in life. Often, we don't know the precarious balance of such treasures. And when they are gone, they are forever lost to the sands of time. Such is the case for our beautiful planet. Humanity has forgotten the balance of cooperative co-existence. We gamble with fate in our reckless co-opting of its bountiful resources in misguided and myopic pursuits of greed. So in the evening sun, our generation must ask: What is the world we wish to bestow upon our children?

Nature's Realm, Tomorrow Child

This is our gift for you
Child of tomorrow's uncertain fate.

You will be the bringer of much, untold.

Awakened thought is but a gossamer thread   in time's forest.

You must heed its trembling concern – as we muted nature's voice.

In the wind, nascent thoughts create tomorrow's realm
it speaks of the delicate fate of harmony's scale.

We, yesterday's stranger, anoint your path
absolve us from our inequities
as we ask you to improve future's legacy.

You are the Stuarts of gifted treasures we squandered.

And nature will now seek from you many things:

Bend within the breeze   and let fall heavy ways.

Flow as one through the river of life.

Take never more
than your soul's memory can retrieve
and leave behind uncluttered paths
for others to walk.

Above everything:

Hold true to the balance of all for all … remains in delicate balance.

Nature itself provides balm to all living creatures. When in the midst of solitary walks, it's then we realize we have never been alone.

Placid Forest

Creaking sounds, bows sway
pine sap memories, fill the air
placid forest walk.

Have you ever found yourself walking deep in thought and suddenly you are distracted and transfixed? It can be an unexpected encounter that mutes the mind and begins an entrancing dialogue with the soul.

Sight of Perchance

In the forest frost
Beauty's secret can unfurl.

Rippled beams emitting
a prismed shimmer
iridescently framed
through disrobed forest arms.

A waterfall symphony
where glaciers crept and churned
creating ledges and spillways
leaving behind fluid footsteps
that bubble and gurgle.

Along a path
the fog glides
upon the forest floor
lingering and curling
sometimes sailing in the muffled air.

Beauty waits for the eye
calling to the soul
it's a dance
of unexpected perchance.

Why does memory's visit bring with it also the sting from yesterday; the sting that often reminds us of failings, unfinished business? Like shadowed creatures, it can be suggested; our fears lurk quietly in our thought's forest.

Things of the Forest

There are many things
in the forest
tonight.

Things of shadows
and lowered voices
moving with nuanced intent.

Many things
in the forest
tonight..

As my years grow long, I often ponder 'But where has life's magic gone?' And then without hesitation, I find fragments hidden underneath a rock or buried deep within hollowed knots of forest trees.

Wintergreen Forest Lore

Wintergreen berries quietly shine
a secret beacon for children's eyes.

Hiding upon the carpet of forest floors
while soggy autumn leaves
soften our walk
for deeper we go, into forest lore.

Enchanted, twisted arms of trees
stretch out to us
as if to beseech
from us, don't leave.

Higher yet above forest floor
fairies and sprites spy in delight
twinkling lights and magical notes
as secret friends of children play.

Children hold carefree court
with magical creatures of all sorts
while ancient magic unfolds its art
before their unburdened joyful hearts.

Oh, aging soul
be not in such a hurry
to leave these lands
sit a while and take pause
...for magic lingers still yet
in wintergreen berries
spoken of in forest lore.

II: Rivers, Mountains and Waterfalls

What is this primordial peace we encounter listening to the gurgling gossip of waters as it moves from powerful pounding, cascading and crashing to gentle flowing, trickling that finds its placid peace? Does the constant abrasion polish not only rocks but also perhaps our inner dialogue as the spray and gentle water vapor cleanses our secret lives? In limpid pools where life seems to find and give root, we can find rejuvenation by allowing ourselves to release, flow and let settle those things that must find their rest. Cast yourself into the frigid mountain waters and let all pretense of purchase find its intended way.

When words can no longer convey, and we alone in the rain stand ... there can only be the rushing river of pain that takes us ... and we must but go.

Droplets

Yet as the rain falls
it drenches in a paradox
its softness nourishes
but its coldness stings.

Droplets of memory
are they Heaven's gift
or do they come and rouse uneasy ghosts?

The freshness of its splash
bursts forth
melding what words cannot say
into crevices where deeper things
are hidden and tucked away.

We are all travelers
on roads of different makings
our hands clasp one another's.

We absorb the warmth of a moment's exchange
snapshots placed in someone's album
and we blend into oneness
sharing things like smiles, picnics, and rides
rides where the wind tangles our hair

... we lose ourselves, courting the wind
and in that swirling mass - we are found and become.

There is change in the winds and sights as nature converses with the silent soul. Yes, the New Year has found us and I feel the stirrings of change.

Mountain Mist

When the cloud's mist
rolls over mountain caps
sounds suspend
and brings to height
the soul's voice.

A chatty one
with much to share.

Oh, could you listen
its mind quite firm.

Bracing breeze of change
whirling through a sleeping soul
that longs yet to breathe
freshness of thoughts
freshness of heart.

When the clouds roll and roar
change is in the air.

Our souls stretch and long
to feel a change of breeze
as the mountain's mist
creeps along the air
flirting with our hearts.

Spiritual enlightenment is a path many find their life's journey reflecting. There are many roads that lead us to our perceived Nirvana, and goodness knows, it is a road with many diversions.

Nature So True

Placid pond of paradise
raw nature in an epic slice
emerald green and sapphire blue
in serene surroundings
we paddle our canoe.

Our destination is unknown
for our future awaits from seeds we've sown
whose course is without correction?
when our humble pursuit
is simple perfection?

I stand in awe of those who seek mountains to climb, finding the ground not enough. I realize for my life, that search is not my call. So while I enthusiastically cheer for those who strive beyond and seek above, for some, finding words can be enough.

Printed Seeds

Bold, was not the name
my spirit chose.

I rode the waves, of those who dared
and marveled at their feat
when victory rang.

But my life, has not been
a shallow grave
in storybooks, of adventure told.

My careful steps, meandered
while watchful eyes
were mesmerized, by life's nitid light.

Perhaps, I might never brace the wind
down perilous mountain slopes
at speeds, that blur the sight.

Rather, I'll pause to ponder
pulling from lofty mistrals
vagrant words, traveling as pinecone seeds
watching as they repose, on thought's pillowed tray.

And, there by chance
might new life emerge
... from printed seeds.

There are stories held quietly between walls, scents lingering long after flowers have bloomed. Like the curling smoke from an outened candle, wafting upward in sinewy ascension – life lingers, fragments, memories ... they long to speak their story. But silence is more than a door that opens and closes to another world, yesterday lodges itself in every crease and fold of time's elusive visage ... can you imagine the stories told?

Stories from a Mountain Cabin Wall

The cushion of summer grass
beguiles my perception's prism
Spring rightfully becomes a fresh banner
another generation defines social evolution and norms.

With fondness, I know so well
the energetic rise of imagined moments
a future whose unfoldment
holds worthy, exalting mankind's potential.

I look through fogged windows
vacillating between yesterday's polished shine
remembering scents of meals cooked and shared
while equally experiencing fullness
as my frame slowly dries – a leaf in autumn's grip.

I feel aches and longing tiredness
to return
from whence my soul sought its adventure of life
the candle flickers and casts shadows I don't fully comprehend.

Aye, I have lived a fullness
I have lived.

Have you ever wondered how ingenuity finds its way into the thoughts of man? Is it contained in an apple that falls from a tree, a Eureka moment of electricity, from where does advancement and clarity bring such knowledge?

Tomorrow's Thought

The mist of never's thought
patiently drifts and drapes

..knowing one day it will arise.

When the careful hand of fate
stirs the curious mind of man.

Self-expression is a driving force within humanity that seeks to give vent to our individual uniqueness and validates our existence. While personal expression is ephemeral, it is never in vain. The act of personal expression is beauty unto itself as lingering remnants continue to enhance humanity.

Vapors upon the Trail

Forest sounds are muffled and low
but crackling leaves spill their secrets
for there within, a presence stirs
while nature takes a quiet repose.

A mist silently rolls,
carefree upon its carpet
unfolding vapors that leapfrog higher into the air
as curious sprites witness
the elegance of its unfurling, wily dance.

To anticipate its form, one has no hope
not even the mist knows its course
caught between fluctuating currents
of dancing elements and serenading energies.

Vapors reticent to leave at dawn
now they cannot help but recede
erasing all proof they once roamed and sailed the air.

But legends of mist's enduring spell
remain intact and are retold
when sprites emerge, to silently spy
dancing vapors upon the trail.

Of all certainties in our world, change can be the most fearful ~ for we never know the form it may take or the price it will exact.

Waterfall

And there I stood
watching from below
while winter's waters
flung itself with abandon
to spring's fertile ground.

So bound does our soul become
often lost in the perfection of change
that goads and prods
in evolution's unfold
daring a soul to emerge ~ from its binding cocoon.

The soul cannot dance
a ceremonial rite of change
until it learns to leap
or is thrown from its perch.

Like a winter's water fall
a soul must release all purchase
and take flight upon the winds
... fragment, if it must.

Allowing every particle of our soul
to swirl freed from any stagnant state
that was locked in winter's grip.

III: Winds, Rain and Storms

Standing in the face of wind, I brace to hold myself still. But my frame is less than the trees that bow and bend to their gusty master. The storms and ravages it brings punish those that hold reluctance as a prideful partner. To be clear, these forces can represent tests ~ examining our commitment and only we can learn of which they are meant. Honesty can be but a true armor we carry to shield as we navigate our way through our tests... for in the bearing of its message we discover whether to stand fast or humbly bow.

The bracing coolness of coastal and forest winds awakens and pulls deep from within our spirit. We often tuck the most painful of experiences into places, meant to be forgotten, and perhaps managed another day. But there is no hiding from death's memory as we walk upon the shores and forest floors ... the winds always find us ... beseeching us to enjoin in deeper conversations.

A Place to Breath

Wispy remnants
tokens of life foregone
as sorrow sends her tears
into the wind.

A bride bound
to the Ocean's breeze
a wound laid open and bare
its sting a melancholic breach

... striped and worn
its soul naked.

Yet, Death bares no intended malice
upon sacred limbs
lost in the grasp of sadness.

But within the desolate desert
of wintered loss
life, still, finds purchase
begging us to breathe
as its winds cradle embers of life.

Withered leaves
we long to breath
seeking grounds upon which we might repose

...while winds continue their haunting flow.

Challenges are perpetual companions in life's journey. No matter the scale of these challenges, overcoming them requires courage and faith.

A Storm Draws Near

In the dawning sun
the sky is set
the horizon portends
a storm draws near.

The clouds all mount
all the seas, they roil
the course is known
this ship must sail.

The sailors know, their chance is slim
yet, doesn't matter, for fate is sealed.

And so this pattern, it does repeat
the moral here, is simply clear.

Tomorrow's sun can only rise
when storms we pass, to seek blue skies.

The sea conjures ancient images of mystery and might; for it is a source of food and flight. In a forgotten fishing town – there are people, who know all too well, the uncertainties of life upon the sea.

Lonesome Sailor Winds

Lonesome sailor winds
howling their course
upon Doolin Bay.

A shadow one can spy
standing upon the cliffs
towering against the sky.

Hair strewn about
by the wind's
tumultuous toss.

While down below
waves they crash
a deafening blow.

Hurried sailors scurry
unloading their catch
for the day has ended
and they seek the warmth
of home's nestling hearth.

But there remains the shadow
upon the darkened cliff
whose eager and plaintive eyes
maintain a vigilant watch.

While the waves continue to roll
another sailor has paid
the ravenous sea
his final toll.

Not everything in life is straightforward. We find ourselves struggling at moments to understand what life might ask from us and where it might also lead. Sometimes all we can do is simply allow time to shed light and provide answers.

Pausing in Life

There are those days
when the soul must drift
carried by winds without name.

The melody of falling rain as it lands upon leaves in trees above, the sudden exuberance of bird song filling the air, the smell of saturated soil ... there's a fullness one can feel knowing life continues in its ebb and flow.

Places Where They Land

In my garden
many tears have watered flowers
they bloom boldly
not shy in splashing colors
nor hidden in coveted spaces.

Slugs crawl
along the gravel path
not mindful of the jagged edges
bruising tender feet.

It breathes softly
expanding
as the rain wets the appetite to live again
birds remind us
from their perched nests

...Life is complete
as its story finds new paths.

Nature continuously reveals her mysterious lessons to the watchful heart. One of life's most readily observed lessons is the concept of cycles and regeneration of life.

Rain Drop Echoes

Listen, can you hear
raindrop echoes?

Quietly now, you must tune your ear
for a silent wisdom, nature shares.

Little raindrop
from darkest skies you were set free
who knew where you would stop?
But the sky was grand, and you sought to see.

You rode a sunbeam
along your way
and stopped to chat
with breeze of wind.

But your adventure did not end
when you met the sea, so vast
you joined right in, your water to blend
as a droplet, your time was past.

No more as tiny droplets to be
their voices now, in unison roars
gentle waves within the sea
... finding new shores.

Every sailor knows fabled stories of the sea; A jealous mistress tempting her lover and claiming his soul for eternity. It has often been said only purest of hearts can withstand temptations and remain true to a dream.

Siren of the Sea

In the most crystal and blue of waters
a mermaid is said to swim
she scours the seas with deepest intent
a sailor to find, a treasure to keep.

With fiery red hair
floating wildly in sea
alluring and untamed, is her silhouette
forever tempting every fishermen's net.

A catch of her gaze
and his fate is clear
to the sea he belongs
no time for a tear.

This tale of caution
does every caption share

…'Keep your eyes on deck
for the sea, may not your life spare.'

There is not one of man that has not of loss understood whose words run deep and cut within our soul. While loss runs deeper than the Earth's very core, nothing is ever truly lost ... for the winds carry more than simply particulate fragments.

The Wind

The wind continues to blow
but it is not a hollowed rush
that rapes the land and steals the soil.

The wind carries the words and hopes
the dreams and gifts
of those who lived and those who left.

The wind that blows
is not bitter or cold
maddened or harsh.

It carries songs from yesterday
while its force is strong, it pushes and pulls
to guide us on to another day.

Don't lament, terry or fret
cling strong to release all matter of fear
though its force dares us beyond.

For look
the wind carries the words and hopes
the dreams and gifts
of those who live and those who left.

Have you ever tried to catch the breeze or hold onto love's precious moments? You've probably noticed such pursuit cannot be contained but for brief moments. Love's moments are meant to infuse our lives with freshness not be contained in staleness: One must move forward in life to welcome love's ever changing infusion of freshness.

Time's Breeze

Breeze, soft upon my skin
while memories cling like sacred charms
holding onto life's wispy branch.

A timeless residue of love
quietly lodges itself amongst fragranced pollen
as my heart secretly imprints its scent
upon my willowed soul.

And the breeze bends the reed
in a field of symphony dance
that only fleeting glimpses might see.

Like a stone skipping on a river's crystal edge
love's moment moves
in sync with time's fleeting breeze.

Silence is a haunted sound found in the wind, carrying ghosts whose nagging presence crawls upward our spins and unsettles our nerves. Why does silence haunt us so? Is it the possibility of being forgotten? Where not even a footnote gives grace to our struggle? Yet, we are left in our aloneness, while we're surrounded by so much noise, activity, and busyness ... Perhaps in dreaded silence our legacy becomes evident in the waves we create, the lives we effect, and how those effects create enduring change for humanity.

Whippoorwill & Windmill Song

Who listens to the whippoorwill
as dust storms pelt the mill's rusty blades?

Its singsong screech mocks the summer skies
as mirages of heat waves bake the hardened clay.

Secluded from eyes
sound is muffled
or does it really have any say?

The Savannah covets and takes away
as desiccated bones litter the desert beach
like fallen jewelry forgotten in its box.

Essence of life
perhaps too insignificant to mark
yet we try in our sphere of influence
to achieve some noteworthy marker of having lived

... trinkets of souvenirs
we place in tended relationships
but the wind continues and blows

... while rusty blades squeak in protest.

Love is the most beautiful and encompassing of all life's joys. And yet sometimes it is fleeting, a passing wave that leaves little behind.

Winds, So Fierce

Wind, why do you blow so fierce?
and with you, my dreams take
my dreams of love, so beautiful was made
it was grand and spread across the sky.

Yet now, fragments only dare linger
wind, why do you blow so fierce?

In my years as a poet, I have tried to express the curious phenomena that occur each time I entered a forest or a nature preserve. It struck me there was a moment of profound transition that happened each and every time. A sort of baptism, a moment of erasing everything that I thought was important from my consciousness. A moment that brought me back to remembrance of where I knew I belonged. A moment of echoes ... carried within the wind's song.

Wind Song Echoes

Ephemeral summons
yesterday's rendezvous.

A child within
seeks its place
where silent salutations
console the withered.

Hidden enclaves of sacred
hallowed grounds of hold
a sanctuary to reprieve an eclipsed soul.

Lifting it to sail
between groves of ancient
and beginnings of birth
where man celebrates the divine.

Winds of time and waves of motion
the distant walk of man
to find things of other.

But we grow neglectful
when we loosen our tethers to nature's moor.

And so, winter's sentient guardian
in its merciful act
gently spreads the frost of forgetful
... blanketing its keep.

Lest we awaken
and suffer pain's remembrance.

Lest we awaken
and remember.

Worries, while quite natural, can often consume and distract us from imagining possibilities. But does the wind hold more than fear in its grasp when it ravages our keep?

Worrisome Winds

Worrisome winds of maybe
sitting on tomorrow's edge
how it is the eyes cannot see
opportunity that awaits, to be set free?

Worrisome winds of maybe
how odd it must appear
we fear your force, without control
yet we hope and open the door.

But wait
there comes a breeze of lifting air
a gentle wave of softest flow.

Courage has said
I can let go.

Worrisome winds
you are no more.

IV: Butterflies, Birds and Dragonflies

Could we but lift ourselves into the air, letting only the breeze and our fancy direct our flight~ like the three spiritual sisters: butterflies, birds and dragonflies. Their mythical association of connecting heaven and earth through transformative rebirth aptly symbolizes our human struggles with adaptation, courage, strength and renewal.

In their sinewy flight of beauty, may we align our mental and emotional concordant voices, bringing us to a refined understanding of self-realization.

The pursuit of beauty tantalizes many during their lives; its pursuit becomes a lyrical siren song of elegance. Thinking man's creative genius is found displayed in museums or architectural monoliths dotting the landscape, we often overlook the sublime simplicity readily available in nature. How ironic humanity could become inured to the entrancing creations of nature – thinking we are not one of its expressions.

Be the Art

I was watching a dragonfly today
as it flew in exuberant movements
it darted, hovered and swirled in the air
one could mistakenly believe
it curtsied in flight.

Its movements resembled
an impromptu cotillion
a boundless execution of melding with currents
being bathed in the sunlight
as the iridescence of its wings and body
refracted spectrum hues.

And in the moment of being blinded
by shimmering colorful lights
I saw a sparkle, like dust kernels
glistening as gold...

How often we miss life's dignified art
of being immersed in the moment
of being embraced by elements
seeking to merge with our expression.

Perhaps our greatest art
resides in simply being
a resplendent articulation as one of nature's child.
And the dragonfly?

I believe I was invited to dance.

When beauty grabs our attention, the observer can become mesmerized ~ believing the moment is a sole expression, standing alone in its singular merit. But perhaps beauty has always been a collective expression and very incomplete when we claim sole ownership of its presence.

Beauty In Its Flight

A feather has no idea
of the gliding flight
it orchestrates.

It has no idea of the sinewy beauty
it creates
while it weaves on waves of wind.

Indubitably, its beauty is twined and bound
within the whims of wind's laminar flow
as it marries with the unison
of a bird's layered wing.

Oh, the imagined life of plainness when fear limits our sight. How often do we pine for beautiful expression when we limit our sights to the ground?

But to Fly

There was a trepid caterpillar
reluctant
to accept its transformation
of unpredicted fate.

For it had heard of flowers
exotic
in lands where breeze was strong
and regal colored butterflies flew.

It longed to perch and sail
in such dreamy fragrant air.

And yet
its body gave no sign of brilliant wings.

It could not imagine
the journey pending
brought from tomorrow's wings.

In its perceived little world
it gave into despair
vowing not to emerge
from its cocooned lair.

The worry and concern
our little caterpillar imagined
as it approached its transformative
death.

... it rather languish and die in certainty
rather than risk its unknown emergence.

Serendipitous and erratic flight, my, life is filled with those dreaded moments. But then there will be other moments that allow us to marvel as simplistic beauty permeates and prances through life.

Fluttered and Sputtered

There is this butterfly
that caught my eye
it wasn't a mysterious moment
where Zen talks through a ringing bell
or where mantras reveal their secret spell.

It was Voodoo dancing in the air
as fluttering wings morphed
into beckoning beacons
allowing my eyes   to sail and dine
on shimmering slices of apples and wine.

And suddenly I heard the message
a Morse code signal
it entwirled my soul with its hesitant flight
in all its dippy and loopy
dancing of delight.

How could I have missed
the brilliance of life's flight?

It's life ...

I've fluttered and flown
sputtered and sown
landed here   while I eyed
a landing over there.

It's the brilliance of life   a paradox of journey
filled with irony's humorous attire
glittering and gliding   shimmering and shining
... when finally we look in the mirror
and proclaim ...   life's unique in its timing.

I remember warm summer days, exploring the woods with my companion poochie. Carefree, no worries ... just my little friend and me. I remember seeing a dragonfly for the first time, wondering how could nature make something so small, almost invisible; and yet, make it so beautiful. It was so small, that was one not watching, they would miss it completely. Perhaps that's how one begins to watch, look ... to find those things we normally miss.

Lazy Dragon Fly Days

Dragon fly dreams
lullaby in its lyrical sing
a lifetime ago
... or so it seems.

Glistening creeks
talkative trickles
removing our shoes
dunking our toes
watching tad polls dart about
in such bygone pleasant flows.

Watching turtles
sun their shells
plop, plop, plop
hearing them
into the water as they drop.

Suddenly, iridescent wafty wings
dart above the shimmering waters
spreading rainbow dreams
and beauty of like
I had never seen.

A flittered presence amongst a field so grande, where color sprays, such a visual demand. Our eyes can surely not resist, to rest our gaze upon their paletted bliss. And so each year, butterflies take to the winds, gathering nectar, pollinating next year's gardens and fields. Can you find yourself snuggly in the midst of a butterfly's beauty as it intoxicates our thoughts and renders our soul ... adrift?

Pollen Prance

Gather pollen's powdery dew
take a breath, flutter & fly
forest eyes and raven's breath
hail your flight, upon the sky.

Tip toe, curtsy & petal prance
a taste of nectar
absorbs you, into a tranquil trance.

Valley highs and prairie plains
boisterously boost of last year's flame
time in essence, in short remain.

Tip toe, curtsy & petal prance
take my breath
.... flutter & fly.

Hope has often been depicted as a white dove. I often wondered why such imagery captures the soul. Certainly, peace is symbolized with white's pureness.

Sacred Wings

Tomorrow's promise
gently flies
carried upon hope's sacred wings.

Kindness is one of the greatest gifts mankind can offer to its fellow creatures. As we continue to expand our cities, let us remember to keep a place for them. This poem is dedicated to a little bird, Harry, befriended upon my windowsill. My sister and I will forever remember his quirky tenacity and joy for living ~ despite his injuries. To our little friend, Harry, may Heaven's skies open wide to welcome you home.

Special Place

There was a place called Harry's home
a special place for birds to roam.

Now Harry wasn't a bird of choice
in fact, if said, an ugly sort
his plumage was sparse, upon his crown
a missing eye was plainly seen.

Time and time, again
Harry came to feed
he made quick friends of fellow birds
all of which shared special needs.

Missing feet or mal-formed claws
battle broken, such slighted birds
they searched to find
safe place to eat.

Time enrolled and others came, too
word had spread so fast around
a special place, for special birds
a windowsill, up off the ground.

Fall winds gathered and then they blew
but little Harry came not to feed
winter's freeze soon settled in
but little Harry came not to feed.

...there was a place called Harry's home.

Fleeting treasure hunts fill many lives, and they manifest in different ways. It's undeniable when we fail to reach our goals that sometimes our loss leaves us feeling empty and deprived, but maybe there are other forces at work – as our loss becomes part of another's story.

Sweetest Berry

Ah, the sweetest berry
often dangles heavy from the longest branch
precariously tempting above the river's edge
as we fixate on our ripened fruit.

Yet, the rushing waters below debate
in such a tone, as if to dissuade
our hasty steps along the bank
… slippery, slippery, our feet now slide.

The imaginary taste of our prize
obscures our vision, luring us further yet
giving us bravery to tempt our fate
but suddenly a fluttered flash
distracts us from our take.

With peering eyes, as eager as ours
a little bird lands upon the berry's branch
snatching the plump fruity jewel.

Hurriedly it flies away, to its nested perch.

But the moment's lament is short-lived
as our feathered friend offers a needed meal
to its insatiate, now quiet, little chick.

Does a flower ever know it is a flower? Does a bird ever know how its song changes and charges the air upon which it sails? Perhaps not, but beauty in its multitude of expressions alone knows it must find its way into our world – and we, the observer, can only marvel when it graces us with its presence.

When a Song Will Emerge

Songbird solo
sitting silent upon your perch.

From where are your lyrics born?

Is it from the sun
whose rays dazzle our eyes
shimmering sequins
strewn above in the skies?

Is it from the wind
secretly courting a flower's prize
misting pollen
in such clever disguise?

Songbird solo
sitting silent upon your perch
watching from afar
hoping, not in vain

... someday your song will emerge.

V: Sun, Stars and Heaven Above

Blinking bright against the darkened silhouette of Heaven's floor, the Sun rests while we reach for more. But what do the Heaven's above and its Constellation of companions pull from within our souls if not for the hope of divine guidance ~ in its unknown form. We squint in the evening's dusky sky, trying so hard to find the first star upon which to cast our lucky wish.. And then we wait: Asking of Destiny to share of our ordained fate, ever hopeful, as our child self from so long ago.

Discovery is a journey that begins and ends with a single step. Yet sadly, many people often fail to begin taking their first authentic steps in livings their lives as a result of disappointments and difficulties.

Anew

Let not the nature
of time's mercurial mood
bring you to a place
filled with sadness or disquietude.

I am told of another day
whose sun shall rise
and in this hope, go forth
claiming life, your prize.

Dreams are often forgotten during one's lifetime. The responsibilities of parenthood can translate into delaying or completely sacrificing aspirations. But the irony of life's detours can often reveal greater unknown dreams.

Captured Stars

It was the Mother's special day
they gathered together to celebrate
their means were sparse, not much to give
but dreams were plenty, and hearts were full.

A little girl, with button eyes
it was her Mother she idolized
her time had come to give her gift
an old shoebox was what she lift.

With careful hands and curious mind
the Mother gazed, intently inside
her eyes could not fully contain
all those things her heart did feel.

In joyous tones of obvious glee
she sat upon her Mother's knee.

I have captured the sky, for you
filled with stars from heaven above
lined in velvet of softest black
with silver pins, to mark the stars light.

They twinkle, when light upon their heads fall
so in the day, you can see them all.

In softest voice, the daughter did say
within the stars, I see my dreams
I brought them here, to give to you
that you might yet, see yours too.

There is a rare exhilaration one finds in special moments of life -when busy thoughts finally find their rest, and a deeper quiet can express its peace: Buried under the noise of daily lives – there it simply waits.

Content

Watching as the sun
takes its daily leave
the warmth of passing years, a paradox
as the chilling evening sets cold
against my skin.

My worthiness of unearned merit
has instead been graced
to fill my life with jewels
magnificently placed.

A quiet reprieve, the beauty
again, expressed
in the day's splendor of setting
brushed across the vivid skies.

Were my life to end mid-breath
I would again, say
balletic gifts I had found
... and I, content
in its express.

Interesting is the path of life and the forces that move us along; whether willingly or unwillingly. Sometimes these very forces buffet us along that we feel so disoriented without a clue where to turn. Despite these apparent moments of vulnerability, a light remains, stretching outward to us, offering us hope … a new beginning.

Eastern Star

Tomorrow's journey
is born upon the breast, of yesterday's dream
when the Eastern Star rises upon morning's shoulder
stretching and reaching, to purchase greater height.

And as its light climbs
the world cannot stand still
it turns and rolls in search of even more
while the Eastern Star fills the sky.

But the Eastern Star is no match
for forces of a turning world
its path, now becomes set in the West
and its light now fades to slight
while adding colors not found in its former eastern port.

As if almost suddenly
only minute fragments remain, to glimmer as light
as the Western Star fades, under evening's watch.

Darkness
then begins to spread its nightly gown, upon the world's floor
and now a different light begins to shine
light brought as twinkles from far away
and upon these stars people whisper
and cast their wish.

From our limited view, it might appear
sometimes our guiding light disappears
but the night's blackness patiently reveals
light is forever, and hope is near.

The Fibonacci Spiral has been referred to as nature's universal code. The familiar spiral shape is found in the iconic seashell. For ages, mankind has been fascinated by this repeating mathematical expression in life and many theories abound.

Eternal Spiral

Ordered patterns of life
expressed in flowers of light
twirling patterns of DNA
and cosmic galactic display.

But of what import
does this golden ratio play
when math itself
leads us to infinity's door?

Fractal spirals
replicating at endless scale
could it be enlightenment's verse

... for life's never ending tale?

How often does light become the vehicle for moments of deep epiphany and connection to life. More times than not, humanity functions in a profunctionary state and it takes a shimmering beam of light to jolt our awareness into the brilliance of life. It's hidden everywhere in plain sight, on forest floors, in waters, in our homes and cities. All it takes is one beam of light hitting our soul 'just right.' And in that instant, we're propelled into an intimate encounter with of awareness ... whereby, we are left never the same.

In the Birth of Light

In the frigid air of solemn
and all its forgotten
light trickles and footsteps on water pearlettes
perching daintily upon woven silken filaments
suspended unnoticed between the changing breeze.

Light searches for surrender and fragments
in places where life summons sparks of resistance.

Desiccated jewels
... scattered.

Petitioned to drape its shimmering gown
upon water's transitional flow
seasoned pieces of life
cautiously grasp for purchase

... while hibernating roots of life
fastidiously rest in the fold of winter.

Delicate silhouettes
courageously summon light's attendance
in this dance of life.

How beautiful does this cycle
ebb and flow
between its state
of darkness and light.

Maybe one of life's benefits is acquiring wisdom? Wisdom in learning to find acceptance of those things we have no control over. Maybe wisdom is finding peace within the chaos of our life's storms? Maybe sitting under a blanket of stars offers perspective not found during day's light?

Sanctuary of Night

Within the night's sanctuary
did I espy this life
its consummate ~ endless expanse
respective tributaries ~ distracting retreats.

No judgment I could conceive
my only intent ~ to heed its course.

In this chasm was found
… a vastness of tranquility
of nothing greater to be found
no fuller sense to be contrived.

One by one … in gradual accord
the lifting vapors of peace they did vanish
and in their stead was to appear
disquieting voices … a crestfallen shadow.

Within the night's sanctuary
… I did befriend this life.

Have you ever found yourself gazing at the night's lovely stars and wondering why its sight fills you with content?

Flickering Lights

Gentle flickering lights
softly encased
in the night's frontier.

Dazzling prisms
sacredly suspended
in memories of yesterday.

Faint traces reminisce
before my eyes
tempting me to recollect.

Hidden amongst so many
yet, singularly brilliant
shiny like a penny.

Barren moments of heart are landscapes windswept where soul and mind find a curious disconnect. Ripe for personal examination, these moments challenge all to reestablish personal equilibrium – a feat not for the faint of heart.

Sunset

The raw emotion of regret
stagnates heavy
pregnant pauses
faded and worn
winter's sunset
left
with nothing
to adorn.

There's an alchemy that bewitches when light and its obscuring occurs. A spark that ignites, elevating latent energies and aspirations ... Suddenly it's there ~ imagination can no longer be bound as we are pulled along into a state of discovery: Light becomes an invitation into something we cannot deny.

Tomorrow Finds Its Way

The sun rises
as we stretch
we long to be
participate, grow, and be seen.

But where does our inspiration
come from?

Are we the makers of our destiny?

Or are we the echo
from a source
we have yet to identify.

VI: Flowers and Gardens

I remember the crunching sound of gravel as my feet sank into the rounded pebbles, the sweet sound of gravel, as I stepped back into my Mother's garden. I was home again, how I missed home. I remember the smell of her flowers, roses were her favorites. How I missed home. In every garden I walk, they are steps back into my most favorite moments of life... where nurture and beauty offer their touch in the deepest recesses of my thoughts.

A winter's day reveals a lonely weed growing through a thick layer of mulch. Against all odds this weed continues its struggle to survive. As this display of tenacity surrounds us, can one feel emboldened within our daily lives?

Aspiring Weed

Aspiring weed
why does the world not see your worth?

Instead they seek to rid your presence.

While most gardens, you will not grace
abundant you grow, in wildest of place.

Yet still, you often encroach in subtle ways
a repeating mantra spurs you forward
'Out of nothing, will something grow.'

A defiant rebel, against all of man's push
you breach the boundaries set, to curtail and contain
no cement or asphalt safe, from your advance.

Aspiring weed
why does the world not see your worth?

Do their eyes sorely miss an obvious sign?
you contain the best of man in your rooted self.

Your desire to persevere, to rise above and shine in light
is the very same echo, found in man's plight.

We are but a part of life's cycle, a transitory expression whose flight encompasses things of hope, joy, love and despair. How soon does this lovely dance bring us to our final breath, as one by one, our fingers softly release their hold upon things our soul tries to cling.

Dried Husk

Dried fruited soul
your husk rustles in the wind
as scavenging wildlife pluck your remnants
their sustenance in frigid winter's lair.

Desiccated jewels once ripe
plump from juices of life's frothy bloom
your sinewy frame, bare branches
they, too, now fall upon the ground

...a lifeless thud absorbed
in the isolated forest hush.

No, I don't think there is much that could pry me from a garden. Each plant has its own intention, each tree meant to shelter its undergrowth ... and I, but a passing inhabitant, that would surely not survive but in its presence.

Every Garden Speaks

In my garden
where little things happen
my eyes greet its visitors.

Like bees dragging their bottoms
carrying so much pollen as they approach the heather
I'm not sure if it's a crash landing or a planned snack.

I think the red iridescent flashes that whiz by my eyes
are really sonic flying Humming birds
dangling Fuchsias discharge their nectar fragrances
and they the least able to resist the drops of tonic.

The little Junko birds seem the ones with most humor
they sit on trellises and find nearby statues to their preferred liking
I imagine their chirps are meant as gaily parlayed greetings
meant to thank me for the spiced seeds brimming in their little feeders.

The waterfall winds past Old Man
an aged Weeping Siberian Fir
the vapor gathers droplets on his arms
and he glistens and thrives
as dragonflies rest on his gracious bows.

It seems we all share secrets
in this hidden garden of life
....
while the rest of the world
busies itself
finding worth in things I don't understand.

Isn't it amusing to realize we spend our years in pursuit of so many important things? And then one day, we understand those things were not so important, after all.

Finding A Garden

There was a walk
I was meaning to take
it took years
to find the place.

A quiet garden
fluttering dragonflies
and leaves whispering answers.

How we can take for granted the gifts of nurture is rather surprising. But for children raised in such environments, how can they know otherwise? Our perspectives are often shaped from limited experiences. And yet, the greatest gift that nature gives is the gift from Mothers ~ who often remain unacknowledged in their efforts.

Flower's Soil

And a Mother's love
can bring the strongest
to their knees ...

filling eyes with clarity
to understand kindness
giving tokens of specific dose
... nurturing lives while creating hope.

It is said
the lotus stirs from the deepest mud
and brings forth beauty none can rival
... this is the journey of a Mother's love.

Gardens contain more than flowers and scents. On melancholy walks during fall, the soul carries on conversations with yesterday's heart. As the leaves waft slowly towards the ground, our hearts feel the heavy absence of fondest touches – voices, scents … life's season closes itself.

Garden Walks

I have found
not yet
the garden that holds eternal
the beauty your presence brought.

Neither the sun, so bright
nor the flowers, with their aroma's delight
match the melody of your sight
there remains an absence
my deeper plight.

Like songs in a bird's flight
wings of today, breeze of tomorrow
only thoughts and mementos
hold your charm so tight.

And all that remains
… illusory glimpses of you
dancing in the breeze
as I stroll
in my garden's reprieve.

Peaceful is the soul that sits and smiles upon life as it offers us its face.

Lotus Blossom

Serenity's sister
shares its peaceful bliss
as quiet contemplation unfolds
and our lotus blossoms,
...unfurling its scented petals.

All the while
in quiet sits
innocence
with a smile
gently waiting
to greet its grace.

Life continuously talks to us in subtle ways: Often offering messages meant to help us make our way through life's journey. Serendipitous gifts are moments of life's reward, and careful eyes enrich the world.

Offered A Rose

Another day began
heavy with dread
though the air was filled
with Spring's joyful reign.

Mindless routine
erased spontaneous' path
and the day let off
same as the last.

But along the way
of morning's promenade
a voice called out
crystal and clear.

With joyful glee, of hopeful youth
an armed stretched out, with flower in hand
the garden was grand, and tended with care
rose bushes abound, spilling everywhere.

In haste
the flowering gift was refused
there were things to do
no time to waste.

Came another day
and the scene did repeat
the doddering lady, clamored about
offering to all, her flowering jewels.

Smiling and waving
people passed her by
yet again, she gently spoke out

Are you sure, you wouldn't like a rose?

Apparent and true
life's message was clear
so many people
yet, fail to hear.

And, so it is
on life's promising path
you never know
when a gift might appear.

So listen close
as I share with you
life offers to all
a garden of sorts.

It's up to you
to watch and see
maybe life offers joy
simple, and free.

When we lose someone to death, it often feels as if the beauty present in our lives is lost forever. But as found in fading notes of song, beauty transmutes and carries on.

Petaled Time

Like translucent jewels
of life's garden
petals and leaves
all fall to the ground
and wither
in their season time.

But vestiges will remain
and cling
to gossamer silken threads
spun within our minds.

Bringing again to life
a flower
in a garden
whose presence
could not remain.

It is easy to be captured by youth and apparent beauty during life. Often we lose sight of beauty found in hardship, aging, and differences: Inherent beauty; however, remains present during all aspects of life.

Promise of a Rose Bud

Do you remember,
the freshness of the rose bud
and its promises contained?

Gently unfolding petals,
hypnotic lingering scents,
... its splendor revealed.

Yet now ~ the day grows long,
and the sun begins to fade,
the rose silently surrenders its beauty,
its petals no longer reaching upward,
... into the dance of life.

Did you notice the wind's forces shaping the rose?
did you notice the dried veins mapping each petal?

One by one, the wind loosens the dried petals,
... falling gracefully to the awaiting ground,
all its energy consumed,
... no more to give.

But do not weep spent flowers of youth,
for beauty and external truth,
... continue on.

Who has never stopped in a field to look for a four-leaf clover? Who has never looked to the twinkling night skies above and wished upon a falling star? Does not the same person admire the dandelion as they cast their wish and blow its seeds in hopeful anticipation? Perhaps hope is the seed we ritualistically send into fate's wind ... hoping such dreams will find root upon nourished grounds.

Wishful Seeds

Simple little rhymes
passing through
innocence in time
casting dreams
upon the breeze
as we scatter
such dainty seeds.

Longing thoughts
careful pleads
launched adrift
our wishful needs.

VII: Fairy Lore and Fanciful Things

The pairing of fairy tales and fanciful things is neatly entwined in imagination's symbolic representation of unbounded adventure. What a boring and unidimensional experience our lives would be without the unexpected spice of imagination, where laughter lightly lingers and colors so bright the unexpected of things not seen. In solitaire, children find friends beyond sight's view, they dance and prance about in gleeful revelry pouring them another tea while adjusting crowns upon their friend's iridescent flowing hair.

Children, they remain the sacred sentinels, possessors of remembrance of this world's sentience as they weave and wave greetings to filamented figures of fairy lore.

Tired, torn and worn, isn't that the story we apply to things of waning interest? This poem offers humor in reaffirming the time worn truth: "One man's trash is another man's treasure. Perhaps there are more things in life that we can repurpose while offering value to others?

Gnome Home

Frolicsome and bejeweled gypsy shoe
you've been encrusted with a mossy glue.

But why did your partner of travel
leave you behind
when clearly there were places
needing to find?

Vagabond treasure, littered and lost
without thought and callously tossed.

But don't crease your brow
and conjure demise's daunting dance
while fairy magic lifts its phantom fingers
to cast its spell of second chance.

Crispy, crackly carpets of leaves
past the brittle bark of glorious trees
comes a curious and cranky, gnarly gnome
looking to make you
his comfy new home.

Imagination is such a playful partner. Can you for a moment conjure such a sight where a little man with a funny hat sits so mysteriously upon his pachyderm? What could he, indeed, be thinking and what sort of adventures have they led?

Pachyderm Parade

What a ponderous plight
perched upon a pachyderm
are you perhaps
patrolling for purple parrots?

Pardon me
but they are a persnickerous pack
as they lack any sort of polite
parading past your pachyderm
clearly lacking permission or tact.

The playful part of ourselves is often throttled as we become immersed in the more serious aspects of life and responsibility. Can you remember looking up to the clouds and finding dogs or cats, or maybe even, finding fairies sitting along a river's brook as you walk in the woods? Wouldn't it be wonderful if we could incorporate imagination into our daily lives, allowing us to keep childhood simplicity and joy within our grasp?

View From A Window

Standing by my window sill
I squint and rub my eyes in disbelief
for what I think I might see
is really quite a big deal.

Floating in the air, in a buoyant bounce
were hoards of bees lifting mighty trees
how does logic defy my blinking eyes
when my mind bends simple thoughts
into such beguiling lies?

But rather than cast doubt on my delirious mind
I laughed aloud and straddled my window sill
stepping onto clouds like stepping-stones
I buzzed with purple and pink stripped bumble bees
then we took to climbing those floating trees.

VIII: Seasonal Serenades

For unto everything is there a season ... a time to live and laugh, to stand in the sun as it shines its warming breathe into our thoughts, where butterflies land on our noses and the birds chirp their songs. And the world spirals in its gentle rotation while the breeze slowly turns, increasing its force and tickling the leaves ... the air sheds its warmth as a crispness envelopes our bare knees. We say good-bye to life's urge to sprout about in all of nature's fields and reach for autumn's tempered hand that yearns to rest. ... Ah, the call of each season's tempest song and how fully it allows us to live.

The crispness of fall's air fills the soul with much reflection. It doesn't matter how many previous cycles of season changes we experience, the reflective tendency finds us all.

Autumn's Avalanche

Silent water drops
scattered rustles, painted leaves
autumn's avalanche.

As summer light yields its dominance and the moon claims its starry field of misty light, autumn crispness signals the closing of life's cycle. During this time, we naturally turn to reflections of life, its meaning and expressions. While many equate autumn with loss, perhaps life's greatest expressions are found at this time?

Autumn's Sanctuary

It is, you know, a sanctuary
a sacred vault
where season's diminishing life
allows us one final brief moment of brilliance
...in the resplendent encounter renowned as Autumn.

A coalescing of pageantry retreat
where the sun's slanting light
refracts in erudite piquancy
autumn shares an intimate kiss.

It can be thought the Universe
in salute to Life, offers the best of its show
displayed in a glitzy choreographed
confetti leaf fall.

Autumn wistfully welcomes the weary
beckoning as it opens its misty dew shawl
but before winter's approaching call
we should dance in glorious Fall.

Doesn't it seem that Fall brings a greater wistfulness to our window as we watch trees gently shed their leaves? Watching colorful leaves fade reminds us poignantly of life's continuing cycle. But if we're not careful, we can too easily forget that from Winter's dormancy there will emerge fresh buds ~ another cycle of life and loss.

Changing Seasons

The seasons do change
and with them they take
the past sadness that lingers.

But perhaps, too, with its changing
does it bring the brilliance of hope in new thing,

... love waiting to be born
and smiles waiting to be shared.

And so I greet this day
with fondness
and an open heart,

... for what things have passed and what yet may.

The motion of a train ride can become mesmerizing as we peer and look out from our vantage point. And sometimes in this day dreaming moment, we find unexpected things. Isn't it serendipitous how our mind slowly brings to us the things we often hide from ourselves?

Far Away

Take me far away
on a traveling train
where forest snow
shimmers in a dazzling display.

Take me far away
where my breath whispers thoughts stray
like vapored cloud
they linger and then float away.

Take me far away
where winter casts its dormant shawl
and I might by the window seat
cast my wandering soul.

Christmas jubilation is contagious and often reveals the hidden child within us all. All too soon, we forget to allow the wonder and joy of our inner child to find expression in our daily lives. And yet, a little walk in Winter's forest can be enough to rekindle such moments of innocent imagination and expression.

Fallen Flake

Special little fallen flake
in Winter's frost
you sought your fate.

Upon a tired, fallen log
by a tiny, mittened hand
magic stirred and magic formed
as you became ~ winter's fine lad.

With such a jolly
and seasonal glow
the little snowman
was finally kissed
… under the mistletoe.

Winter's approach is long felt in the soul before nature brings forth its frost-bitten mornings to our door. Is Winter's slumbering perhaps a retreat where tomorrow's dreams find their beginnings?

First Snow

Soon Winter will put to sleep
all of yesterday's glorious feats
and birth new dreams
we've yet to meet.

Impermanence marks all aspects of life, and is beautifully captured in nature's brilliant displays. So perhaps in our haste to rush forward or remain behind, we can embrace the energizing moment of change.

It Must Pass

I could trickle and flow
down the river's path
I could sway and blow
amongst the forests, so vast.

But the moment, cannot remain
it must pass.

Grains of sand, on desert's floor
pebbles so smooth, on river's bed
forgotten mementos
of time's wearing hands.

And all of these
they must pass.

No moments can best, the force of time
they all must flow, and find new place.

For I am time
and all must pass.

Skip a stone and jump a puddle. Land on a crack ... you're in trouble. Hop scotch and bubble gum, snow cones and sitting in the sun. Life, a trip, a Sunday drive, sticking feet in woodsy creeks ... making friends and having fun. ... Childhood daydreams become our favorite things.

Long Ago Days

Bemused and befuddled
by
beckoning, babbling bumblebees
beyond the flotilla
of falling leaves
Fall brings
its
flirting breeze
...
unfurling ubiquitous undulations
of
seasonal tease.

There is a timelessness in which our thoughts seem to reside, from which our wisdom seems to emerge. Is it possible a residing commonality units our understanding of eternity with nature's rhythms?

Mind's Time

Wander through the space of time
wander through this mind of mine
fluid thoughts flow
through the course of time
naked branching thoughts revealed
through this mind of mine.

Recently I witnessed an individual openly disparage another from its clan on a media forum; spewing vitriol as contempt extended destruction's clawing arm. And I thought how small the bitter world of an ailing soul, reaching out a spinning and snaring web of anger ~ it can only be a slow death one makes for oneself.

Scavenging in Yesterday's Winter Grave

Long the shadow cast
of gnarled naked branches
from a barren tree
as its dead limbs creak in the wind
in winter's muffled pallor.

Words from acid's bite
feast on yesterday's footsteps
leaving but residuals
of regret and misunderstanding.

But the snows are coming
and will bury such impetuous acts
promising the blanket of forgetfulness
and leaving bones to gently rest

...in graves not of their making.

Can you remember the special of Spring ~ even as your body does age? It's easy to forget the soul's conversation with Spring while the years so quickly pass, but fragrances from yesterday's flowers will always return.

Spring's Song

There was a song
I remember as a child
I did sing.

The words escape me now
and only pieces of the melody
can my thoughts refrain.

Fragmented tapestries
of a childhood gone.

The magic remains, yet
as I stumble to recollect
all of memory's words
where yesterday and youth
played so well.

Time carries a special seasoning
a precious flavor
where my heart of old
savors as if anew
the morsels
of yesterday's dew.

As the sun sets
and the stars begin their shine above
we think of time, my friend
those glorious and wonderful Springs
for children of new
and those of yore.

Spring is a magical time when all of nature experiences an unexplained exuberance. After Winter's long slumber, life once again shrugs its laziness with newfound energy and force.

Spring's Spell

Such a crafty art
contained in Spring's spell
bringing in new life
from seed's dormant well.

Barren limbs, are bare no more
the hope for life is budding forth
surfacing here, and over there
sprouts of green, they're everywhere.

Opening the window, of morning's door
the air is crisp, inhaling deep – we want some more
a beckoning scent begins to waft
it sails so soft and tastes - like a purple grape.

A splatter of colors galore
find their way upon our garden floor
flutter, flutter, butterfly wings they flap
while bees all buzz, for pollen's allure.

So hurry, scurry, and run to play
the spell of Spring, has come today.

Simplicity of childhood moments resonates forever in our adult hearts. Those memories are the moments that give balm to our aging hearts. Can you recollect the simple and fond memories of Summer's night and the joy deeply contained in those quiet dark nights?

Summer's Night

Along the rocky coast
of Blarney Bay
sits a field of verdant green.

Where nights so sweet
the lullaby of Cricket Lore
begins to sing.

Night's shimmering gown
glistens of distant light
beckoning forth the dreamer's voice.

Softly, the crickets call
summons remembrance
from an ancient root.

And the world stands still
as a forgotten child's heart
again finds its beat.

Flying amongst fireflies
the dreamer finds its light
and leaps again, into the symphony of life.

Years do pass
so quickly by
but within all hearts does remain
remembrance of Summer's night.

Autumn carries a similar energy as spring; the hustle and bustle to prepare for nature's transformation. How often do we join in this ritualistic celebration?

Winter's Blossom

Frisky squirrel's tail
hide and seek, nuts bounty found
winter's blossom falls.

The rhythms of life carry a cycle of reflections and winter contains its unique call. While most of life is retreating in slumber during this time, our thoughts bring back memories of year's past. Often our reflections bring melancholy matters to mind; but are there new promises yet to be realized in awaiting blossoms found in spring's coming?

Winter's Sojourn

Every season must advance
its progress, we cannot withhold
the winds begin to dance and whirl
arousing Winter, his cold to unfurl.

Plants reluctantly will bare themselves
while animals instead must insulate
this winter's a time for deep retreat
our minds, they seek to ruminate.

And in the dark of Winter's grip
dormant lays promise of Spring's arise
days slowly will increase their breadth
the sun, too, shall restore its glow.

Until at last, snow begins its retreat
its waters shall quench the Winter's parch
with buds anew and flowers galore
our soul's awake to live some more.

So do not mourn this Winter's gloom
for Spring comes next, with plenty of bloom.

IX: Poignant Pearls

Hidden amongst our thoughts, in such cluttered rivers of talk, we barely hear the voice of clarity. But the grain of sand has begun its work as we slowly add balms of soothing reflections to bring to perfection crystal thoughts layered in iridescent understanding. These pearls we add, one at a time, to our life's library and perhaps we are asked to share these little gems with receptive ears.

I often think without nature's beauty we might easily drift between islands of mundane and disregard.

~

.. Could I again sit in yesterday's garden and linger within its beauty ... may we carry such treasures through the long years of our life.

~

The morning sky loudly declared – and all of brilliance and possibility were brought to my feet.

~

Winter silently sojourns while dreaming of spring.

~

In yesterday's mist lingers the treasure of youth.

~

Kindness is one of the greatest gifts mankind can extend to its fellow creatures.

~

A heart that loves all of nature is its child.

~

There are those days, when the soul must drift, carried by winds without name

~

A little feather's journey
finds its way
to land upon a lovely flower
in my garden...

~

How can I not be joyful? ....
It's the little things in life that matter.

~

Possibility has perched itself eagerly upon morning's breath ~ where knowing has yet been left untouched...

~

There is a timelessness in which our thoughts seem to reside, from which our wisdom seems to emerge.

~

Simply hearing a truth … will create a momentum all its own.

~

Write to wonder … and your words will awaken hearts.

~

My soul is rooted in love … and will no longer be directed by fear.

~

I am willing to accept the changes occurring in my life,
I will release any anger or disappointment,
I choose to allow these changes to transform me
… into a stronger, wiser and more compassionate being.

~

What fears will you explore today?

~

Fare thee well, most noble and true friend …

~

Pictures, they are the heart's vault … where we store our treasures.

~

The years wear long while the heart's pain remains so fresh …

~

In my words … I find your memory lingering.

~

Truth is a burden for the bearer. Often its words ~ better left unsaid.

~

An inquisitive mind opens the doors for those who cannot imagine beyond the door's boundaries.

~

An inspired heart never stops its talk – until it stops its beat.

~

No one is immune from a broken system whose floor is littered with ruins of dreams.

~

Full self-expression is necessary to compliment humanity's diversity

~

When we disenfranchise any segment of society, we rob humanity of great accomplishments.

~

Once we release our words, they continue and imbue blessings upon the ears and hearts ready to hear.

~

Our heart's words are often the most spontaneous and welcomed.

~

Random kindness is never lost on the receiver.

~

Love is a beautiful encounter preserved in time's gentle hands.

~

In solitude, does our soul often find its peace.

~

Our circumstances hinge upon chance and its meeting with us.

~

Wisdom is a long road with a sense of humor.

~

I like to think of poetry's opening sentence synonymous to smelling the cork from a bottle of wine freshly uncorked ... the story is built on this first important impression!

~

It's amazing the opportunity life presents us to view with different eyes; circumstances are often the lens that provide such moments.

~

A well-worn face is a life thoroughly lived.

~

The apparent is only seen by those with sight.

~

Our muse must often journey on its own … in its solitude … to gather words, to gather insight, but the spark of inspiration always returns to its keeper – our soul.

~

When we see our work through another's eyes, we expand our ability to express ourselves in a more varied manner.

~

Maintain your unique style – for the world needs diversity to experience the full range of beauty's presence.

~

There are walks we take that forever change our path. ..Walks that bring in fresh air to free our soul, and wisk away its stagnant state.

~

There exists sufficient beauty
residing quiet and calm in collective souls
to nurture the hungry world
with seeds of hope.

~

For eyes that see ... trust always extends its hand, waiting for another to reach out and accept its touch.

Acknowledgments

Finally I can bring to light those people instrumental in shaping who and what I am as a poet. I am most grateful for the unparalleled support from my magnanimous husband, Frank. He has spent more hours listening to my poetry than any person should ever be called upon. He is the gem in my life, and I thank him. I would also like to acknowledge my sister, Anna, I couldn't imagine a better sister to share my life. She challenges me to live and be the best of who I am.

Throughout my writing, I have been fortunate to have such a wonderful group of supporters. I sincerely thank Shirley Bolstok, an established and prolific poet, for her consistent encouragement. Through her nudging, I began earnest efforts to explore poetry as a means of healing. I also thank Patty Bran, Nancy Mesler, Lori Kleppner, Geri Hendricks Trumpor, Maureen Morrel, Shirley Schmidt, Judy Kaan, Diane Wellington, Laurianne Sorinson, and Shannon McGlon, my core supporters. I thank all my Facebook fellow poets who have shared gracious compliments and support along the way – allowing me to refine my craft: Vickie Rebb-Seeley, Valormore DE Plume, Raja Williams, Eva-Marie Kuhne Wehrman, Eden Hundsdoerfer, Audley Hitchins, Marcella Leff, Sue Lobo, Nancy Hall, Melvin Little, Gerald Darbeau, Peter Forster, Michele Joyner Flowers, Anthony Lynch, Nancy Crossland, and Vera Biddle. I will add a note of additional acknowledgment for those that were not included.

A special thank you goes to Adam Taylor for the wonderful cover photo. Thank Adam Taylor and Shirley Bolstok for editing input. And for the crowning editing polish, I extend my sincerest gratitude to John Herlihy. John taught me the importance of precision in preparing and presenting my manuscript. In addition, I am most appreciative for those who took the time to provide reviews for my first book in the Wandering Wonderer series: Brenda Lee Ranta, Shirley Bolstok, and Gerry LaGuardi Leonard.

Every author speaks in glowing terms about his/her publisher, and without a doubt they deserve this recognition. But I need to share with my readers the 'rest of the story'. This book has been in the making for almost 5 years. During my entire 8 years of writing poetry, Cyberwit has encouraged and supported my efforts consistently with Anthology and Author activities. As I recognize and thank them for publishing my first book, I am also thanking them for all those years of believing in my message and timing.

About the Author

Baidha Dominique Fercoq is a poet, short story writer and artist. Topics for her poetry center mainly on nature, love, loss and social issues. Sketching, painting metal art and wire sculpting are additional venues she enjoys. Expanding her poetry presentation Baidha initiates artistic collaborations with photographers and musicians whose works focus on nature and her healing capacity to create poetry videos.

While also writing to social and political injustices, Baidha is especially known for nature poems speaking to her ability to nurture, mend and inspire. It is Baidha's sincere hope that speaking to such topics can broaden awareness and assist others in being an active presence for the betterment of humanity and nature. Fascinated in the stories behind a poem, Baidha began including prose vignettes to enrich the experience of each one.

The highlights in her poetry include being nominated in 2018 for the Pushcart Prize by Creative Talents Unleashed, recognized in Sweetycat Press's Who's Who of Emerging Writers 2021, and receiving the 2021 William Shakespeare Poetry Award. She had multiple poems published in Cyberwit Anthologies, Creative Talents Unleashed, Pegasus Literary, Sibylline Magazine, WildFire Publications, Spillwords, All Poetry, and the Scarlett Leaf Review. Baidha remains active in many Facebook poetry sites and has been an Administrator for Poetry In My Mind since 2015.

Educational pursuits such as a BS in Healthcare Administration and an MBA in Global Management were instrumental in providing intimate perspectives into how business and the balancing of rich interpersonal experiences leave a majority of people unfulfilled and marginalized personally and economically. These experiences provided Baidha with the basis for becoming a voice for the disenfranchised and those wanting to connect with their intuitive voice.

Baidha currently lives with her husband in the Pacific Northwest and can be contacted at BaidhaFercoq@gmail.com.

To view additional poetry by Baidha Fercoq, visit the following sites:

YouTube Channel and Facebook Page- Baidha Fercoq

www.ingramcontent.com/pod-product-compliance
Lightning Source LLC
Chambersburg PA
CBHW022157160726
48282CB00024B/234
* 9 7 8 8 1 8 2 5 3 7 2 2 4 *